A Packet of Poetry

by Caroline Molyneux

GOLDEN QUILL PRESS
Publishers Since 1902
Manchester Center, Vermont

Golden Quill Press
Manchester Center, Vermont

© Caroline Molyneux, 1996

Library of Congress Catalog
Number: 96-76076

I.S.B.N. 0-8233-0508-2

Printed in the United States of America

A Packet of Poetry

To my family.

Contents

My Love

When sorrow shades your lovely face
And stills the pleasure of your smile
Your eyes reveal an inner grace
That my sad thoughts beguile.

When joy awakes your puckish grin
And laughter dances in the air
Your eyes reveal the steel within
And I, your courage share.

Such contrasts, cast
   in beauty's mould
All facets of your life enfold
And in the world, fresh,
   true and kind
I live again, in love
   enshrined.

Fun

Fun is the criteria for having arrived!
Today you are politically correct!
Modernity the sin of boredom.
The attitude of cool,
Who cares, a shrug.
Nothing to do,
Who gives a shit.
No life, no spirit, no love.
Everyone so rude.
Nobody cares a little bit.

Bliss

Sitting sheltered on the porch
Whilst it rains.
A steady drizzle after drought.
Hearing the plants lapping their elixir.
The shining wetness of the grass.
A bottle of Chardonnay, a glass.
This is happiness for me, and
An unfamiliar book to hand.
Is this Paradise to be?

On A Brief Visit to Austria

A tiny country–prosperous–
Clean and neat in every street.
National costumes worn with pride–
On bus or train an honour ride.

Fast flowing Salzach–chestnut-lined.
Schloss guarded slopes, terraced and vined.
Here Richard Coeur de Lion was interred
Until Blondel's freeing song he heard.

Helbrun–garden of playful fountain.
Swaying cable car up Untersberg mountain.
Exploding guns cross Salzburg–round after round
   –St. Rupert's Day proclaims the sound.

Mozart country–Fuschl Lake.
Sacher torte most delicious cake.
The Danube–lunch on board–
A monastery at Melk we toured.

Vienna musical city of Strauss.
The glorious State Opera House.
Teatime concerts in the park,
The city's magic after dark.

The mighty Hof–a nation's past–
Of royalty whose power didn't last.
Baroque churches, ornate, to heaven climb.
Demel's for pastries, gluttony a second time.

These are just minutest bits
Of what is known as Osterlitz.

The Natural Way

The garden had been forgotten.
For years no interfering hand with nature's plan.
No clipping, no digging, no pruning,
    no mowing...
Just growing, and growing, and growing...
A joyful wilderness.
Flower beds strident
    with purple willow herb on the march.
Roses, stalky tall, trying to compete.
Over all humming summer bees replete.
Once naked stone paved paths are ivy dressed.
Dandelions proud, yellow-helmeted
    stand guard.
A bird bath moss-grown, greenly stagnant,
The axis of activity.
Realm of birds, feathers water sprinkle,
    beaks dipped.
Tangle of convolvulus watches
    the patterns of flight,
Pink trumpets blowing a welcoming call.
Trim lawn, parade ground neat,
    no longer shorn;
A field of grasses; wheat,
    red-gemmed with poppies,
Waving free. The scented breeze making kites of the
    butterflies.
Protector of this plot, unruly privet hedge.
No regimented bush.
Sprouting branches proclaiming
    pride of ownership.
Oak and ash, watching tall.
Sentinel.

A Marriage?

The cawing of crows reminds me of England...
On a cold and frosty day–so far away.
I miss you my Land–my place of birth–
My special Isle–
I'll be here awhile.
But home I'll come to rest,
I'm blessed!

I enjoy life on two continents.
America's the new and
Europe the old.
One brassy and bold,
The other weary but still struggling.

Hold hands, you two,
I know
   you'll make
   it through
To the
   21st century,
If you try
   to remain
   true
To each other
   and the
   principles
You both hold dear.

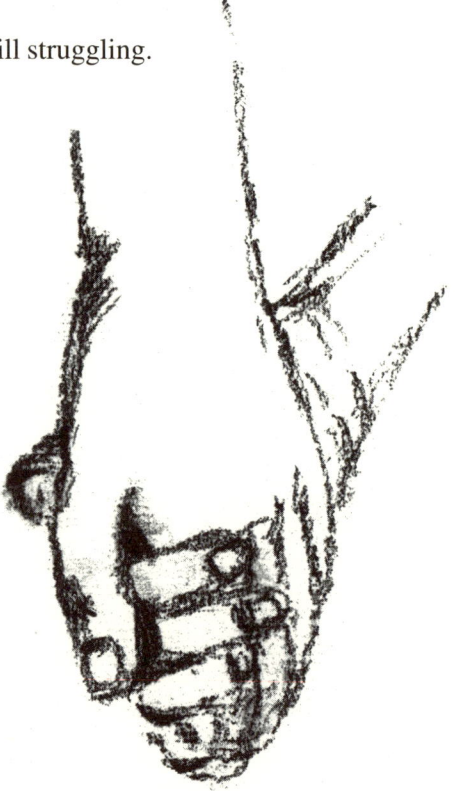

To freedom, honesty and the right
To live in hope and harmony
And never fight.
Keep your conscience clear and
Try not to fear.
Let's solve our problems
In a gentler way,
Learn that tolerance, persuasion
And reason, can win the day.
I pray.

For you England...for you America.
That in your arms one day I'll stay.
I love you, England.
I love you, America.
Be kind to one another.

Deli

Calm down
Coffee in a paper cup.
Bagel with buttered side.
  A sip.
Cigarette a light.
The day is coming bright.
Roads sanded on the way.
Snow flurries early, start the day.
Awake at four thirty
To be prepared for the op.
Left eye, a cataract to be removed.

Blue collar workers all around
A man with flask a bus to catch
He hurries out–a word we snatch,
"Hi, how are you?"
White collar workers
Hardly say a word,
"Good morning."
They act as if they hadn't heard.
Jogger waits in line,
Green top, red sweats.
A Christmas color–fine.
Kids off to school,
Await the bus,
Caps on back to front
Dark glasses, another stunt!

Today no sun,
Why the cap on back to front?
"It's comfortable this way,"
They say.
Their talk of life as though it's worthless.
Large youth, he says,
"Four people dead within days,
A friend from high school, murdered,
Rival gangs, machine gun fire."
Meanwhile my husband lies inert,
His eye fixed open,
Staring at the work, the surgeon,
About to get a new intraocular lens...
Can proceed.
I hope indeed.
"Raising Lazarus" I read.
Has this seed of cataract been sown
Through us to others in our line?
Time will show.
Time to go.
Another day my life to lead.

The Male Animal

Living with the male animal
Is disturbing...
It's his background noises...
That offend.
The unseemly loudness
Of a nose being blown.
The piggy grunts in sleep.
The resonant and rhythmic snores.
The release of air.
A torrential piss
Cascades into the toilet bowl
Splashes onto the metal heater,
Spotting it with rust decay.
The nose being cleared.
The swallowing of phlegm.
The smacking of lips after
An especially tasty meal.

The heavy eater.
The garlic greeter.
The satisfied release, a fart.
Who'd want to be a tart?
The breath after beer.
The sexy leer.
His snorts, grunts, burps and farts
Which are so difficult to bear.
Make living close with him,
No fun, we fear.
Yet somehow, we love
And hold them dear.

The Mushroom Gatherers

Early morning, dew upon the grass.
Mushrooms springing at their feet,
Fast fed through nights by cows,
That patient breed, who grazing feed.
Black faced, ask, what do you want?
My milk? My mushrooms?
Chewing as they follow,
The morning gatherers mushroom browse.
Gentle lowing says, take my milk,
Is it for you, spurting from the udder,
Fresh like the dew and the mushrooms too.
But the gatherers of mushrooms
Do not heed the cow.

With baskets heavily light-laden
They chatter home, across
   the buttercupped fields.
Trailing dewy footprints, home to breakfast.
Mushroom omelette, fresh baked bread,
Hot crisp from all night oven,
Spread with golden butter, jam or marmalade.
Tea and coffee with milk from a bottle
Goes into the cups.
And the cow still waits.

I belong on two continents.
My life straddles the Atlantic.
"Hi!" "Good morning."
"Have a nice day. You're welcome."
"Will this rain ever go away?"
The telephone rings twelve times before reaction.
Four times and a machine springs into action.
Hold open a cupboard, close a closet.
Turn off a tap, turn on a faucet.
Bashed bumper, fender dents.
Write with a biro, use a Bic.
You throw up and I feel sick!

Thanksgiving Grace

We give thanks to our Lord
from whom all blessings flow.

We give thanks to our families
for all the love that they show.

We give thanks for this dinner
that we share today.
And we remember with love
all those far away.

We give thanks to our hosts
to Louise and to Brett...
For this special meal and
rejoice here together
for the happiness that we feel.

Amen.

A Prayer

I pray today, December the 29th, 1994

Oh! Lord help us to be like you–

To be brave and strong
yet gentle and kind.

Help us to save this planet Earth
and all mankind–

Help us to love and to be true
to ourselves but most of all to you.

In Jesus' name–
   Amen.

Hazards of a Jogger

I jog at steady pace,
Towards me comes familiar face.
"Is it pleasure or punishment?"
He asks, bespectacled grin.
"Bit of both," grunts my reply.
"You plan a marathon to win?"
A chuckle and he goes on by.
Speeding motorist
Selfish pass.
I raise my fist and jump on grass.
Barking dog.
ON and ON and ON I jog…
Keep this up wind, rain and fog.
Summer's heat the hardest slog.
Blue jay squawking in a tree,
Mocking laughs at me.
Over the bridge;
Across the field.
Brambles, meadow-sweet, wind waving
In hedgerow greet.
Snails and pebbles 'neath my feeet.
To aching legs I shall not yield.
ON and ON and ON I jog.
Sniffing hound trails after me,
Growls most threateningly.

Lifts his leg against a tree.
Makes me feel the need to pee.
Cyclist coming from the rear
Startles me.
Flashing by so suddenly.
Their approach you never hear.
No panting breath for them
They just change gear.
Branches give a welcome shade.
The pace begins to fade.
ON and ON and ON I pound.
Why do I make this daily round?
To be the healthiest corpse
Set in the ground?
Snap! Yelp! Achilles tendon gone.
No marathon, this year, I've won.

The toxins are coming out
from years before–my body
speaks–through me and shouts.
"Let us out!"
Healing is harmony–
It would help to be a pair.
You hurt me deliberately?
You rarely say "sorry"
Or show that you care–
You put me to the brink of despair.
And don't understand why or how
You put me there.
You are not very kind -
And it seems you want me out of my mind -
Would it make you pleased
Once more–
To have those white-coated attendants
Walk though my door–
A hospital and HELL for me,
Weeks, days, hours of misery.
NO! No more.

I'm so tired–
Sleep comes but scarce.
My eyes sting–
My hands are weak–
My nose is red and sore.
NO! No more.

My throat is parched and dry
And I limp.
The side effects.

My anger throbs and burns–
The drugs are coming out.
Shut behind bars like a criminal–
My crime to be ill,
They say I'm sick.
Shot through with electric jolts–
Like a criminal.

My crime to be sick.
Diagnosed a manic depressive.
Like Dickens, Churchill and their ilk.
But I am treated
With no respect, no loving care
As though no human there.

I'm a loving mother of four.

This pain is hard to bear.

My husband, once more, when I need
Him to understand, to be kind
And sympathize–
Turns callous, cold and
Seems unaware that he is not
There for me–

I need his care, to share this load.
He gives at the office...
For all to see–
But me...me...me...

Ferments this state of
Differences and hate.

I need a hug, a kiss
The certainty of bliss–
We've shared–when you cared.
I need you on my side and
By my side,
For unity, for family, for Happiness
FOR ME.
FOR US.

Square

A square is one who plans in detail.
Everything in black and white.
Monochromatic.
No emotional identity.
No initiative, careful not to fail.
Feelings reined in tight.
No courage to declare.
To take a stance,
For fear of seeming ridiculous.
Proud to be a square.
Why take a chance?

What Is It With Men?

They are so domineering.
Stop telling me how to do,
How to think, how to be.
Take care of yourself.
You've done a rotten job so far.
Get yourself a real doctor.
Not a quack,
A charlatan,
A money maker,
Like Dr. Lack.
You need a caring carer,
For a primary physician.
What a farce! Ever open purse.
Doctors in it for the money.
Hospitals that kill not cure.
Pain and indifference, you'll endure.
Undernourished, underfed...virus bait,
And this is not a problem in my head.
Go in there and you'll be dead.
Robbed into the hearse.
Don't wait.
It's not too late.
Good nutrition–
May put you in reverse?

Patience

The state and quality of being patient.
Waiting, waiting, waiting...
To endure without complaint.
Steadiness and perseverance
In performing a task or a duty.
Sufferance.
Permission.
A species of plant Impatiens...
Anxious to spread its seed.

Steadiness like a rock.
A quality that Peter had.
Quietness or self-possession
Of one's own spirit.
Resignation to His will...
    be done...
Patient Lucy.
Busy Lizzie.
Impatiens.
Patience.
Let it be with me.
Patience won.

Pouring rain umbrellas up
People soaking, dripping hair
Sculpted to head, await
Wet but happy.
Anticipating in the rain
Riding on the train.
Ten minute wait.
The Green Line to the Hub.
Coins are rattling,
Quarters, dimes,
A dollar seventy-five
Jumping around as if alive.
Fed into the greedy maw
The ever hungry machine
Like an animal without a claw.
Riding into Boston on the T.
In bound train for me.
RESERVOIR, a mother, child in arms.
RIVERSIDE, her baby calms.
BROOKLINE VILLAGE, an elderly man
With braid over one ear
And beard, his bag reads
Filene's Basement.

He's dirty and very bent.
LONGWOOD, girl in yellow slicker,
Looking like a fisherman,
Steps off, hood up.
She splashes her way through puddles.
The train draws on
And she is gone.
Improvements on the track.
We wait…will I be late?
A sign reads–
"Creating jobs for today
Better service tomorrow."
Houses draped in vines,
Flower beds.
We wait, excited talking from the back.
KENMORE, a group alights to take a tour.
A black man sleeps, leaning head on hands.
FENWAY PARK, no one needs that stop.
Here there's baseball after dark.
Downtown Boston just a hop.

Litterbugs

Litterbugs who toss their garbage...
Cans, bottles, styrofoam cups...
Who drop their rubbish on the street.
Smokers, drinkers are the worst
Abuse their bodies and the ground...
Empty packs, butts, bottles all around.
At your feet.

Leave it in the park...
Or toss it from their car...
Near and far.
Can have no pride in themselves;
No pride in their surroundings;
No pride in their Country.
Their homes must be a mess;
Their lives a shambles.

They can be likened to a dog
Who feels the urge,
Defecates where he is.

Only, they are worse.
A dog knows no better.
They who treat this planet
As though it were a dump
Don't deserve a space on Earth.

Their Heaven a trash can...
In a garbage dump!

Nora

To the Matriach of my family, Pickup,
Who is 91 today, Dec. 11, 1994.
Nearly a century have you been,
Many wonders have you seen–
telephones and televisions, too,
aeroplanes, automobiles and computers
to mention just a few.

All that time you cared and shared
your love and humor with us all.
Two major wars and a world wide
with many fights and wars.
You've lived in peace and helped
and heard the call.

You've seen the rocket to the moon.
Women leaders of their country,
Who, this century just got the vote.
Many children's lives you've
touched and taught.
Fame you've never sought.
Your parents knew you were a boon.

Your nieces and nephews (quite a few)
Love you.

I hear them tell of recollections
Of your kindness.
Your sisters-in-law, for you,
Had an ever open door.
You taught me to read and knit
and swim, as well.

You've helped in family life and death.
You've been a source of strength–
The hub within the family wheel.

Our love we send on this special day,
and we pray that you'll be here awhile
to stay Great Nora–
in the words of a family child,
so we can visit you another day.

Chairs

On November 24th, 1994
Brett gave us a wonderful present.
Two chairs that he had made
Especially for us.
Adirondack chairs–
No fuss.

You sit proudly there
On the porch
A pair, HIS and HERS
A gift with loving care
Made by our son-in-law.
A solid, comfortable, outdoor,
Unique expression of his pleasure
In the wedding that we gave him.
Thanks to us. His present.
A June bride beyond compare.

Now a pair.
In winter chill on screened-in porch
They proudly stand.
A sleight of hand.
I banished from their lovely home,
Sip on tea and have a smoke.
What luxury our chairs evoke.
I am a queen upon her throne
Put there by my daughter's caring husband.
What a bloke!

Leave them out in winter cold.
In the sleet, snow or rain.
BOLD.
I shall sit upon my throne,
On many a future day.
Happiness a sunny ray.
Thanks to Brett.

Tapir

Strange beast
Brazilian tapyra
Half dog, half hog.
Of the *genus tapirus indicus.*
As a pet they would cause a fuss.
Living in tropical America
Or the Malayan peninsula.
How do they choose such varying abodes?
They have flexible snouts,
To their forefeet four toes
And three to their hind.
Why, no one knows!

Naked with plated skin
Armored with brown behind.
They feed on plants.
Move about at night,
Have a nocturnal rite.
Cousin to rhinoceros.
The size of an ass,
For an heraldic beast they would pass.
Shaped so strange, tapir,
You'd cause a horse to laugh.
In the animal kingdom
You are God's farce.

Hands

His hands are large.
His hands are strong; yet
Gentle hands you'd trust
Could do no wrong.

Hands that can a table make,
Hands that bread most ably bake.
Hands that can fashion a guitar,
Hands that strum a tune or pluck a bar.

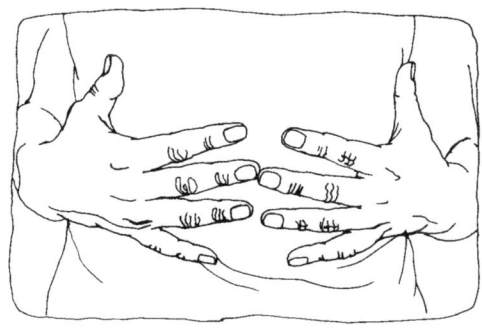

Seaman's hands that knots can tie.
Doctor's hands to soothe a baby's cry.
The hands to hold me,
to caress me, to belong.
In those hands my future I do give,
The hands with whom I choose to live.

Sadness

In the mornings
Early hours, alone.
I lie crying in my bed
For the animals that have been
The friends of times past
The family pets.

Pussy Willow injured by a car
Surviving in the woods
For two weeks until
I returned from a UK visit
Calling...searching...
She suddenly appeared
In the garage open door
Wretchedly thin, blood soaked,
Coat matted, alive.
But in so much pain.
Gently I laid you on the sofa
Fed you warm milk
Talked softly to my striped
And gentle tabby.
She purred and purred
Through all that pain.
"I love you baby,
You made it home to me, again."
What did I do?
I took you to the vet.
Who cruelly examined you, said,
"Internal damage, so severe, no hope."
So you were dispatched.

I cannot forget or forgive myself
For doing that to you.
Beloved pet, who shared my bed,
My life, who liked my lap.
You should have been allowed to die
At home curled up on the chair.
At last content, and me right there.

He put you to sleep.
I carried you home.
No furnace for you.
Back to the garden where you liked to roam.
Your domain.
A hole in the peat, pine scented ground
Under the hemlock.
I placed you there,
    And said a prayer.
      Your mark a rock.
        "Happy hunting
         and God bless."
          I'll see you in
           the great beyond.

Double Standards

Work, the almighty dollar.
Ethics have gone down the drain.
Money, money is all too plain.
The bottom line might soon
Cause the extinction of the human race.
Worship money, greed, Baal.
Charity no more.
Money is the modern whore.
The Earth is ravished, raped, defiled.
Species lost without a trace.
Never can they be replaced.
Poisoned by the enormous yaw
Of pharmaceutical companies,
Chemical companies.
Corporations with no ethics.
Big business tooth and claw.

The animal kingdom, the beasts,
Do not commit the crimes, that man, by
Money, greed and power possessed
Amassing fortunes, seizes, feasts.

Standards in the home, expected,
Upheld by women.
Nurturing their young
With kindness, compassion,
Tolerance and hopes.

Big business grasps, hurts, perverts and dopes.
The bottom line will overtake.
So farewell to the human line.
Guns, chemicals, toxins in the food and water.
Medicine that poisons not restores to health.
All in the name of wealth.

Nature, Mother of all Earth,
Giver of Goodness,
Let us heed thy ways,
Before the cold, cold nothing of the tomb.
Before they seal our doom.

Take The Train

I like to watch the countryside flash by
Sitting in comfort on the train.
A majestic cathedral on the hill,
A mighty castle, turret of stone,
Its keep still stands.

Glimpse a view of snow-capped hills,
And dales with sheep, farming lands,
Each ewe has two, a pair of lambs,
Play hide and seek.

Drifts of daffodils, bursts of yellow gorse.
A cloudy squall and driving rain.
Red brick farm, ploughed field and sturdy horse.
A cutting through primrose and bluebell banks.

A crossing, white gates, whistle shrill.
The train speeds on whilst traffic waits.
The cars and drivers eager to be gone.
Lorries bearing heavy loads; children wave.
Northward the train moves on.

Hump backed bridges, canals
    with painted barge.
Our conductor speaks, on the intercom,
"Next stop, Carlisle, change here
    for Windermere."

Edinburgh City I'll see in a while and
My daughter's greeting, a happy smile.

Manners Maketh Man!!

Why does nobody say "pleasc"?
Why does nobody say "thank-you"?
In the past with ease and grace
These words, they had their place.

"I want." The modern child declares.
His parents smile, his little face,
Grim with need, he should be told
He's much too small to be so bold.
So demanding, and yet so wee...
What will he want at twenty-three?

A $5.00 Day!

I went to the city today.
New York.
$5.00 train ride from Tarrytown.
$5.00 cab ride to the Atheneum Press
Gone out of business.
$5.00 cab ride uptown to the Met.
Closing at 5:00, no success.
$5.00 glass of Italian Chardonnay at
Cafe Grazie.
$5.00 lecture at 6:00 pm
Standing room only.
H.R.H. Princess Michael did us proud.
Catherine de Medici (to whom she's related)
"A Lady Hating in Waiting."
$5.00 cab ride to the theater Gershwin.
A much larger crowd.
A spectacular "Show Boat."
No $5.00 seat here.
This is New York.
I'm broke!

Simply Delectable

Sipping coffee, outside,
   in the cold.
Because I smoke.
A table on the sidewalk.
Shoppers, business types
   passersby.
No one gives me the eye.
   I'm lonely.
A stranger in a foreign land.
I'd like to talk or chat
Pass the time of day...
I may never come again this way!

I bought two books
To keep me company,
The art of Munch and Guterson.
At nearby table she does sit.
    Eats and reads. A readaholic.
"What book do you have?"
"A Hired Gun." Some fable.
"Are you enjoying it?"
"Oh yes! I''ve never read it."
She quickly buries her head,
    Back in the book.
How many people today read anything once?
Let alone twice.
    (I ask myself)
She doesn't want to talk.
I have to go.
Cars park and move away.
The coffee a dollar and a dime
    I paid.
I'd been happier to take a walk.
For no one wished to pass the time,
Or had anything to say!

Advice To You Gents!

If you need to wet,
Use a toilet. Carefully.
Try to replace the seat.
Be considerate and neat.
If you have to explode,
Please go on the commode.
If you want to drain,
Try to refrain,
From doing it in the open,
Or out on the plain.
Sure add to the rain.
Do it on the train,
But only in motion.
Take a leak by all means,
Avoid the peas and the beans.
Gentlemen, if you have any sense
Never piss on the electric fence!

Excuse me, please.

Greeting

Just a card to say "Hi!"
To my cutie pie.
My summa girl...
An apple in her mother's eye.
Watch she's working on
A Wang or IBM computer,
A laptop or a Macintosh.
They're all the same to her.
To me they're Greek.
Happy to search and seek
A modern Ms enjoy
A word processor her toy.
My whizz in finance control (her).
She's my second pearl.

Seal

Oh! to be a seal.
Exploring land and ocean wide.
A ton of flesh reveal,
Playful on the Baja tide.

Harbor seal hugs the coast.
Fights for his right
Master of a harem boast.
8,000 lbs. and 20 ft. of might.

Eats fish and gives them chase.
Roams Baja to Alaska shore.
A rocky ledge his home and base.
His dominance a mighty roar.

Thick layer of blubber
Insulates cold seas, no care.
In water graceful, no landlubber.
Swimming strong, but needing air.

Five toenails relates him to the otter.
100 lbs. at birth.
Needs a sturdy mother!
Talkative, gregarious, flipper flap his mirth.

Hunted for his fat and fur.
Hunted for his ivory tusk.
Man his only predator,
Massacres his babes at dusk.

Wedding Toast

To Jim and Kate
Hurrah at last an honest mate!
(Eric told me to say that).
We are gathered here to celebrate
Your wedding day.
In your marriage we wish you happiness.
In sharing your love and life
Be kind to one another, keep your own identity,
Be tolerant and enjoy those differences
Which make a man a husband
   and a woman a wife.
Savor the closeness and
   the quiet times together.
Be proud of each other's success
And be a comfort in distress.
Remember that the worse often comes
   before the better!

And we know you'll never live to rue
   those words "I do."
We wish you health and plenty of wealth.
We wish you joy.
And for ourselves we wish you a girl and a boy.
So raise your glass up-standing be
And drink a toast with me–
"Today, we unite the Gibbins and
   the Molyneux family.
To Jim, our second delightful son-in-law,
And to Kate, our second lovely daughter–
   Good luck, God bless
And all our love be with you in your
   future married state.
   I give you, Jim, my Kate."

Place And Time

Lincoln
Newark Castle
Rolleston
These names chime like bells.
Fiskerton
Bleasby
Thurgarton
Lowdham
Historic stories tell.
Burton Joyce
Carlton
Nottingham
Beeston
Leicester
Battles and conflicts were fought.
South Wigston
Narborough
Hinckley
Nuneaton
Bedworth
Coventry
Power of kingships sought.
Cities and towns, village and dells.
The past they hardly ever mention...
Known only for their railway station.

A Homemaker's Lament

It is tough being a housewife
You gear your life to their activity
You become a non-entity.
You are D's wife or P's ma,
You lose your own identity.
And everywhere you drive the car!

Daughter in your room when
    you want to dress.
Husband hands you his shirt to press.
"Hon, where are my socks?"
"Mom, where's my coat?"
You're the keeper of the family trivia.
And everywhere you drive the car!

Fill the lunch box, hope it won't go to waste.
One peanut butter, one salami, one for ham.
Rush to school bus in disorderly haste
Grabbing their homework, hear the door slam.
"Seeya, Ma. Have a good trip, Pa."
And everywhere you drive the car!

On the 'phone when you need to call.
They've been together all that day
What ever do they find to say?
To their friends for a movie date,
Across the town, to walk, too far.
And everywhere you drive the car!
Why do all their things end up on the floor?
Why do they never close a door?
Take a shower that lasts an hour?

In the clothes you want to wear,
Leave them dirty–"Is that some tar?"
And everywhere you drive the car!

Meet them in the rain
From choir or football or ballet practice.
Drive him to the train.
Meet him at the airport–the 'plane is late.
An hour to wait. Should you try the bar?
And everywhere you drive the car!

Week-end comes, they're sleeping late,
The breakfast dishes until lunchtime wait.
"A coke! You're not going to eat?"
"Don't want food in all this heat.
Mom, take me to the pool,
    I told Jen we'd meet."
Get out the car, back in the chauffeur's seat!

You need some help to cut the grass,
You need some help to wash the car,
You leave the vacuum in their room,
Invitingly you prop up the broom.
No one heeds your plea,
They're too enthralled by the TV.
Now they drive your car.

They turn your order into chaos.
But when they've left
How you feel the loss.
The end of motherhood.
You're bereft.

Ageing

Bodily functions are such a chore.
The mouth an ever open door.
Washing and dressing is such a bore.
The eyes need help to read.
The ears miss what should be heard.
The memory is often blurred.
Nothing can be done at speed.
Old age is not for me.
I have no choice...
It has to be.

My Place

Does the city never sleep?
Give me the peace of the country.
The gentle weep of the willow.
Do the lights never dim?
Sickle moon peeping over the rim.
Does the noise never stop?
Countryside sounds
The growth of snowdrop.
Sirens wail and taxis toot.
The country call
The owl's hoot.
Give me this tranquil place...
Far, far from city's hectic pace.
Too much noise and too much human race.